GREAT KEYBOARD SONATAS

Domenico Scarlatti

Series IV

Dover Publications, Inc.
New York

Published in Canada by General Publishing Company, Ltd., 30 Lesmill Road,
Don Mills, Toronto, Ontario.

This Dover edition, first published in 1993, is a new selection of sonatas from
D. Scarlatti, Opere complete per clavicembalo, edited by Alessandro Longo, as
published in eleven volumes, 1906–08, by G. Ricordi & C., Milan. The table of
contents and the concordance have been specially prepared for this edition. The
Publisher's Note appears here exactly as it does in Series I, II, and III of the Dover
edition of these sonatas; see that Note for further bibliographical information.

Manufactured in the United States of America
Dover Publications, Inc., 31 East 2nd Street, Mineola, N.Y. 11501

Library of Congress Cataloging-in-Publication Data
(Revised for vol 3–4)

Scarlatti, Domenico, 1685–1757.
   [Sonatas, harpsichord. Selections]
   Great keyboard sonatas.

   "A new selection of sonatas from D. Scarlatti, Opere complete per clavicembalo,
edited by Alessandro Longo, as published in eleven volumes, 1906–08, by
G. Ricordi & C., Milan"—T.p. verso.
   1. Sonatas (Harpsichord)
M23.S28L65   1986   85-752072
ISBN 0-486-24996-4 (ser. 1)
ISBN 0-486-25003-2 (ser. 2)
ISBN 0-486-27583-3 (ser. 3)
ISBN 0-486-27600-7 (ser. 4)

PUBLISHER'S NOTE

This Dover edition of the later keyboard sonatas of Domenico Scarlatti reprints the musical texts from the edition prepared by Alessandro Longo in 1906–08. Scholarly research in more recent times has shed considerable light on keyboard practice in the Baroque era. It is obvious that the Longo edition, pioneering and monumental though it was, preceded such research and did not have its advantages. Longo conceived his edition for performance by the piano in place of the original instrument, the harpsichord. The edition thus includes traditional pianistic markings—the use of pedal, slurs, staccati, dynamics, including crescendi and diminuendi—as well as ornamentation now generally considered inappropriate; moreover, Longo's absolute indications of tempi were foreign to Scarlatti. The suggestions of phrasing and contrasting dynamics lie within the music itself rather than through explicit indication.

This is not to suggest that these sonatas can be played only on the harpsichord, but the performer on the piano should endeavor to approach the historical style as closely as possible. In the interest of providing an affordable edition, however, the pianistic elements of phrasing, dynamics, and pedal remain as they appear in the Longo edition. (The actual notation—pitches and lengths—is reliable and beautifully engraved.)

The performer desiring to understand more fully the interpretation of these sonatas is urged to consult the definitive study, *Domenico Scarlatti*, by the distinguished harpsichordist and scholar Ralph Kirkpatrick (Princeton University Press, 1953; paperback edition published by Thomas Y. Crowell, 1968), with particular attention to chapter 12, pages 280–323, on "The Performance of the Scarlatti Sonatas."

The numbers assigned to the sonatas in Kirkpatrick's study are used throughout the present edition. Following is a three-way concordance of the Kirkpatrick [K] numbers, the Pestelli [P] numbers (from Giorgio Pestelli, *Le sonate di Domenico Scarlatti: proposta di un ordinamento cronologico*, Turin, 1967), and the Longo [L] numbers (from Alessandro Longo, ed., *D. Scarlatti, Opere complete per clavicembalo*, Milan, 1906–08); only the sonatas included in the Dover edition are represented in this concordance.

At the end of each sonata will be found a statement, in full or in abbreviation—C.V., C.S., or E.O.—indicating Longo's source for the musical text. The Longo edition was based upon three sources: (1) One of the two complete fifteen-volume sets of manuscript copies made by a Spanish scribe. The copy Longo used—designated C.V. by him for Codice Veneziano—is at the Biblioteca Marciana, in Venice; the other copy is at the Arrigo Boito Conservatorio library, in Parma. (2) Italian copies in the Santini Collection—designated C.S. for Codice Santini—including five volumes now at Münster and seven volumes, once the property of Johannes Brahms, now at the Gesellschaft der Musikfreunde library, Vienna. (3) The edition of thirty sonatas published in London in 1738 under the title *Essercizi per gravicembalo*—designated E.O. for Edizione Originale.

Kirkpatrick	Pestelli	Longo	Kirkpatrick	Pestelli	Longo	Kirkpatrick	Pestelli	Longo	Kirkpatrick	Pestelli	Longo
396	435	110	416	454	149	436	404	109	458	260	212
397	325	208	417	40	462	437	499	278	459	167	S14
398	493	218	418	510	26	438	467	381	460	378	324
399	458	274	419	524	279	439	473	47	461	324	8
400	228	213	420	352	S2	440	328	97	462	474	438
401	436	365	421	459	252	441	375	S39	463	512	471
402	496	427	422	511	451	442	229	319	464	460	151
403	437	470	423	455	102	443	376	418	465	406	242
404	489	222	424	374	289	444	441	420	466	501	118
405	438	43	425	426	333	445	468	385	467	513	476
406	509	5	426	500	128	446	177	433	468	507	226
407	521	S4	427	464	286	447	191	294	469	514	431
408	350	346	428	353	131	448	261	485	470	379	304
409	403	150	429	439	132	449	405	444	471	327	82
410	372	S43	430	329	463	450	422	338	472	475	99
411	351	69	431	365	83	451	366	243	473	355	229
412	463	182	432	465	288	*454	423	184	474	502	203
413	416	125	433	440	453	455	354	209	475	319	220
414	373	310	434	498	343	456	377	491	476	427	340
415	175	S11	435	466	361	457	442	292	477	419	290

Longo	Kirkpatrick	Pestelli	Longo	Kirkpatrick	Pestelli	Longo	Kirkpatrick	Pestelli	Longo	Kirkpatrick	Pestelli
5	406	509	151	464	460	288	432	465	427	402	496
8	461	324	182	412	463	289	424	374	431	469	514
26	418	510	184	454	423	290	477	419	433	446	177
43	405	438	203	474	502	292	457	442	438	426	474
47	439	473	208	397	325	294	447	191	444	449	405
69	411	351	209	455	354	304	470	379	451	422	511
82	471	327	212	458	260	310	414	373	453	433	440
83	431	365	213	400	228	319	442	229	462	417	40
97	440	328	218	398	493	324	460	378	463	430	329
99	472	475	220	475	319	333	425	426	470	403	437
102	423	455	222	404	489	338	450	422	471	463	512
109	436	404	226	468	507	340	476	427	476	467	513
110	396	435	229	473	355	343	434	498	485	448	261
118	466	501	242	465	406	346	408	350	491	456	377
125	413	416	243	451	366	361	435	466	S2	420	352
128	426	500	252	421	459	365	401	436	S4	407	521
131	428	353	274	399	458	381	438	467	S11	415	175
132	429	439	278	437	499	385	445	468	S14	459	167
149	416	454	279	419	524	418	443	376	S39	441	375
150	409	403	286	427	464	420	444	441	S43	410	372

Pestelli	Kirkpatrick	Longo	Pestelli	Kirkpatrick	Longo	Pestelli	Kirkpatrick	Longo	Pestelli	Kirkpatrick	Longo
40	417	462	355	473	229	427	476	340	473	439	47
167	459	S14	365	431	83	435	396	110	474	462	438
175	415	S11	366	451	243	436	401	365	475	472	99
177	446	433	372	410	S43	437	403	470	489	404	222
191	447	294	373	414	310	438	405	43	493	398	218
228	400	213	374	424	289	439	429	132	496	402	427
229	442	319	375	441	S39	440	433	453	498	434	343
260	458	212	376	443	418	441	444	420	499	437	278
261	448	485	377	456	491	442	457	292	500	426	128
319	475	220	378	460	324	454	416	149	501	466	118
324	461	8	379	470	304	455	423	102	502	474	203
325	397	208	403	409	150	458	399	274	507	468	226
327	471	82	404	436	109	459	421	252	509	406	5
328	440	97	405	449	444	460	464	151	510	418	26
329	430	463	406	465	242	463	412	182	511	422	451
350	408	346	416	413	125	464	427	286	512	463	471
351	411	69	419	477	290	465	432	288	513	467	476
352	420	S2	422	450	338	466	435	361	514	469	431
353	428	131	423	454	184	467	438	381	521	407	S4
354	455	209	426	425	333	468	445	385	524	419	279

*The Longo edition does not include the two sonatas designated K.452 and K.453 in the Kirkpatrick edition, hence their absence from this concordance.

CONTENTS

NOTE: Kirkpatrick's 452 and 453 do not occur in the Longo edition.

Sonata in D Major, K436

24 - a) Nel C. V v'è il ♯ al *La* della mano sinistra.   *En el C. V. tiene un ♯ el La de la mano isquierda.*
Dans le C. V. nous trouvons les ♯ au La de la main gauche.   In the C. V. there is the ♯ to the *A* of the left hand.

Sonata in F Major, K437

6   Sonata in F Major, K437

Sonata in F Major, K438

Sonata in B-flat Major, K439

C.V. Libro X, N. 22.(i)

Sonata in B-flat Major, K440

C. V. Libro X, N. 23. (i)

Sonata in B-flat Major, K441

C. V. Libro X, N. 24. *(e)*

Sonata in B-flat Major, K442

C.V. Libro X.N.25.(e)

Sonata in D Major, K443

Sonata in D Minor, K444

C. V. Libro X, N. 27. (e)

a) Nel C. V. mancano le legature di valore.

16 — 18 (e 73 — 75)   *Dans le C. V. les liaisons de valeur manquent.*

En la C. V. faltan las ligaduras de valor.
In the C. V. the ties of value are missing.

39 (e 41) — C. V. b)

88 — C. V. c)

90 — C. V. d)

Sonata in F Major, K445

Sonata in F Major, K446

Sonata in F-sharp Minor, K447

(60)

(65)

(70)

(75)

(80)

C. V. Libro X, N. 30. *(e)*

Sonata in F-sharp Minor, K448

C. V. Libro X, N. 31. (e)

Sonata in G Major, K449

C.V. Libro X, N.32.(e)

Sonata in G Minor, K450

27 — C. V.

Sonata in A Minor, K451

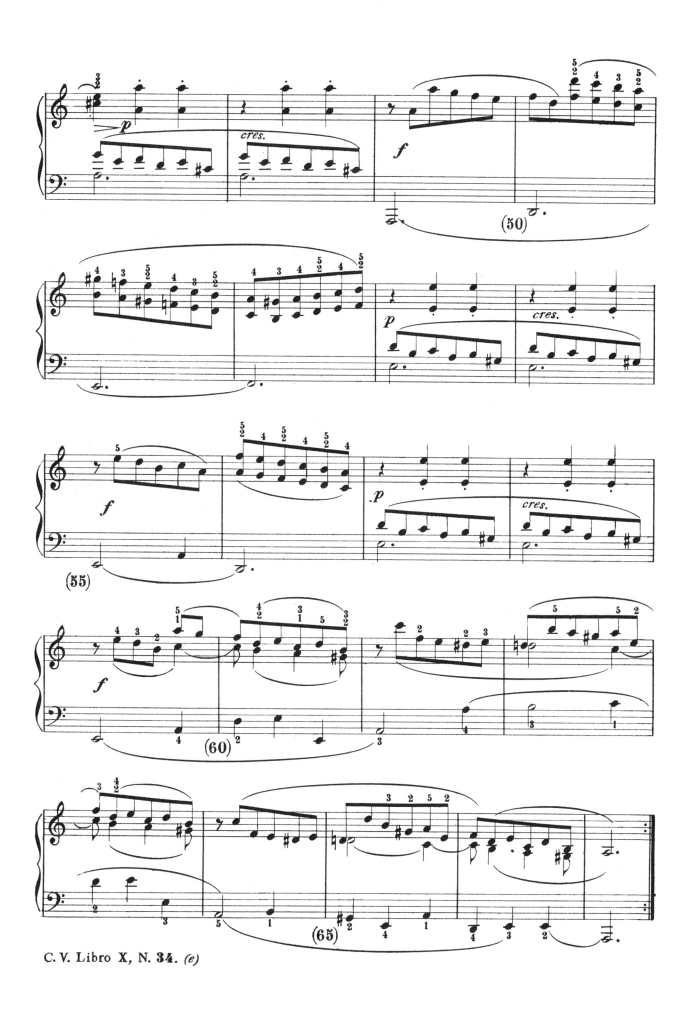

C. V. Libro X, N. **34.** *(e)*

Sonata in G Major, K454

C. V. Libro XI, N. 1. (e)

Sonata in G Major, K455

Sonata in A Major, K456

C. V. Libro XI, N. 3. *(e)*

48 – C. V. *a)*

Sonata in A Major, K457

C.V. Libro XI, N. 4. *(e)*

11-12_C.V. *a)*   **25**_C.V. *b)*

37-40_C.V. *c)*   **54**_C.V. *d)*

Sonata in D Major, K458

C. V. Libro XI, N.5. *(e)*

Sonata in D Minor, K459

(80)

(85)

(90)

C. V. Libro XI, N. 6. *(i)*

Sonata in C Major, K460

(145)

(150)

(155)

C.V. Libro XI, N.7. (e)

Sonata in C Major, K461

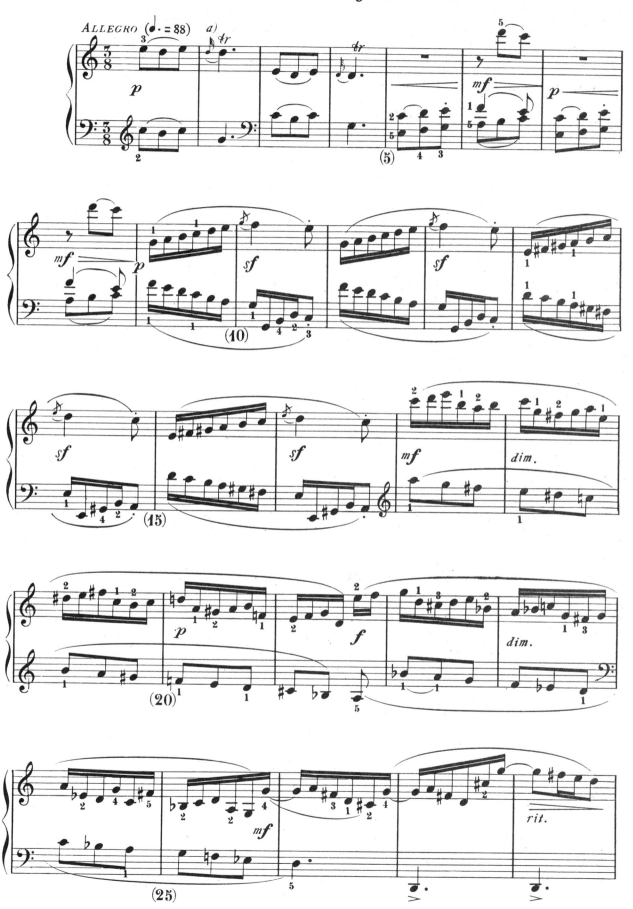

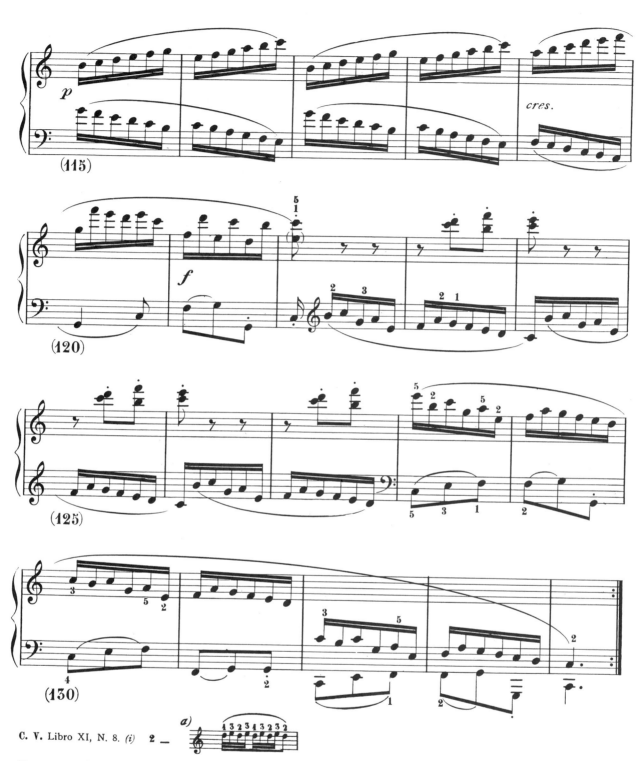

(115)

(120)

(125)

(130)

C. V. Libro XI, N. 8. *(i)*   2 —   *a)*

55-94 - *b)* L'episodio in *Sol min.*, costituito dalle prime venti misure della seconda parte, vien subito riprodotto in *Do min* Tra l'uno e l'altro si notano piccole varianti che non mette conto ridurre ad unica formula: meno che nelle misure **91** e **92,** delle quali dò il testo del **C. V.**

L'épisode en Sol min. formé par les vingt premières mesures de la seconde partie, est tout de suite reproduit en Do min. Entre l'un et l'autre on remarque quelques petites variantes qu'il ne vaut pas la peine de réduire à une version unique sauf dans les mesures 91 et 92 desquelles je donne le texte du C. V.

El episodio en Sol menor constituido por los veinte primeros compases de la segunda parte, se reproduce inmediatamente en Do menor. Entre uno y otro se notan pequeñas variantes que no es conveniente reducir a una sola fórmula: menos en los compases 91 y 92 de los cuales doy el texto del C. V.

The episode in *G min.*, formed by the first 20 bars of the second part is immediately reproduced in *C min.* Between one and the other there are slight variations so that a unique formula is not necessary; except in bars **91** & **92** of which I give the text of the **C. V.**

c)

89 (e 91, 93) _ C. V.

Sonata in F Minor, K462

Sonata in F Minor, K463

C. V. Libro XI, N. 10. *(e)*

Sonata in C Major, K464

C. V. Libro XI, N. II. *(i)*

29 – C. V.   *a)*

67 – C. V.   *b)*

Sonata in C Major, K465

Sonata in F Minor, K466

C. V. Libro XI, N. 13. (i)

a)

5 _ C. V.

Sonata in F Minor, K467

C. V. Libro XI, N. 14. (i)

18-21_C. V.   77-80_C. V.

Sonata in F Major, K468

Sonata in F Major, K469

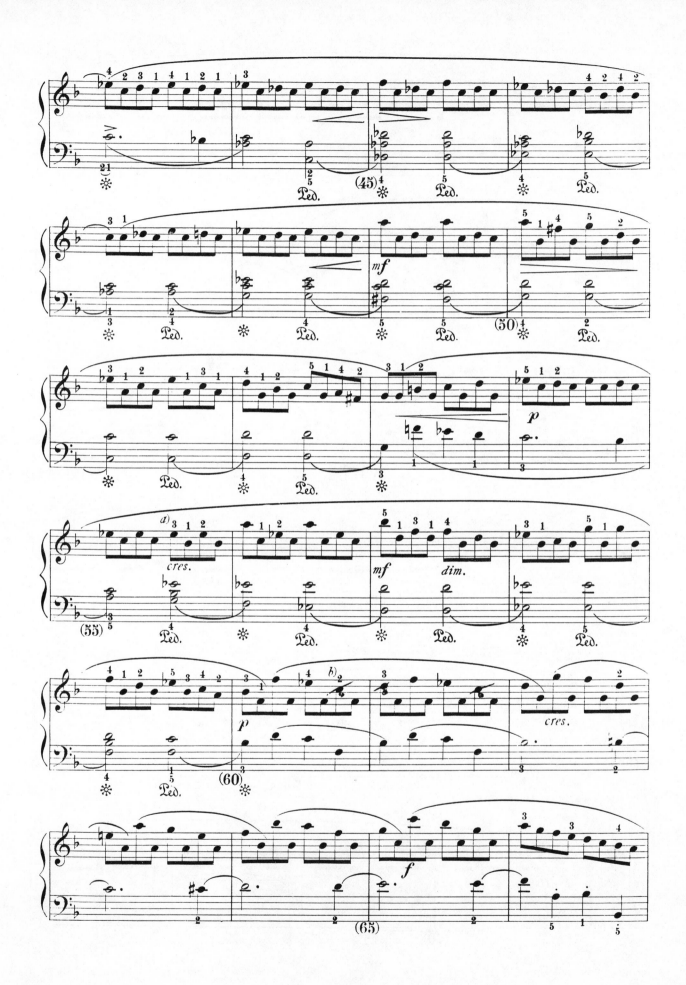

Sonata in G Major, K470

C.V. Libro XI, N. 17. (i)

Sonata in G Major, K471

Sonata in B-flat Major, K472

Sonata in B-flat Major, K473

(85)

(90)

(95)

(100)

(105)

C.V. Libro XI, N. 20. (i)

Sonata in E-flat Major, K474

Sonata in E-flat Major, K475

Sonata in G Minor, K476

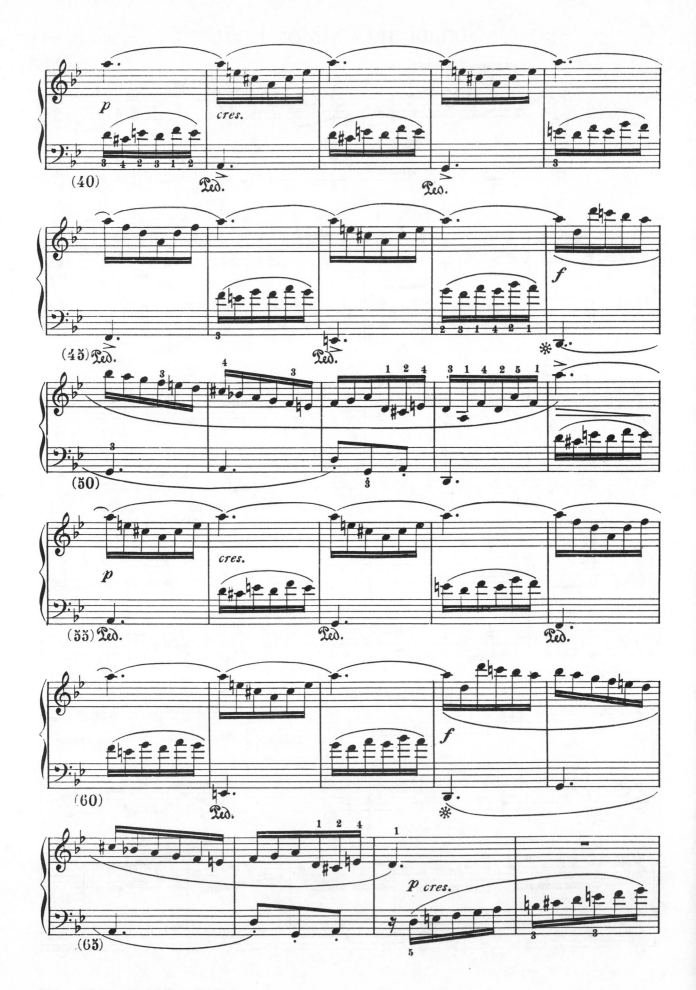

C. V. Libro XI, N. 23. (e).

Sonata in G Major, K477

C.V. Libro XI, N. **24.** (e)

15-17_C.V.

82 c)Nel C.V. questa misura è duplicata.

80_C.V.